AF361835

The Ultimate
Polar Bear
Book for Kids

100+ Amazing Polar Bear Facts, Photos & More

JENNY KELLETT

BELLANOVA

MELBOURNE · SOFIA · BERLIN

ISBN: 978-619-264-034-7

Imprint: Bellanova Books

CONTENTS

INTRODUCTION

Polar bears are one of the most majestic and fascinating species on Earth. Their fluffy white fur and playful nature in the snow make them all the more loveable.

Join us in exploring the world of the world's furriest marine mammal and deepen your understanding of these beautiful animals.

Are you ready to embark on this journey of discovery? *Let's begin!*

POLAR BEAR FACTS

Polar bears are found in the Arctic wilderness in Alaska, Canada, Norway, Greenland, and Russia.

· · ·

Polar bears have a layer of fat called blubber, which helps keep them warm in sub-zero temperatures.

In the town of Longyearbyen in the
Arctic Circle, it is a legal requirement
to carry a gun in case of polar bear
attacks. However, you can go on trial
for murder if you kill a polar bear and it
was not in self-defense.

. . .

Male polar bears are called boars.
Female polar bears are called sows.

. . .

The polar bear is the only bear that is
a true carnivore, meaning it only eats
meat. Most other bears are omnivores,
meaning they eat both plants and meat.

Time for a swim!

A polar bear's stomach can hold up to 150 lbs. (68 kg) of meat at once!

• • •

Polar bears can smell their prey up to 1 km (0.62 miles) away and smell a dead seal through 3 ft (91cm) of ice.

Polar bears are the largest species of bear. Male polar bears weigh around 992 lbs (450 kg), while females weigh between 330-550 lbs (150-250 kg).

...

Polar bears are the only species of bear that are marine mammals.

...

Polar bears are listed as a vulnerable species. Their populations are declining as sea levels rise and the ice caps shrink.

*A polar bear crossing the
Arctic tundra.*

Polar bears spend much of their life hunting, but only 2 percent of their hunts are successful.

. . .

Although polar bears prefer to eat seals, they will also eat other marine animals, such as walruses, whales, and small fish.

. . .

To survive, polar bears rely heavily on a diet rich in high-fat content foods, primarily seals.

. . .

A polar bear's stomach can hold 15-20 per cent of its body weight.

Female polar bears can be up to 50 per cent smaller than male polar bears.

. . .

Polar bears are only found in the Northern Hemisphere.

. . .

Scientists can extract the DNA of polar bears just from their footprints in the snow.

. . .

Most species of bears are born without any fur. However, polar bears and giant pandas are the only bears born with thin white fur.

Hybrids between grizzly bears and polar bears exist. They are called 'grolar bears' or 'pizzly bears'!

• • •

Polar bears living in northern Canada are most at risk — their populations are declining primarily due to habitat loss.

• • •

All bears are great swimmers, but polar bears are the most efficient swimmers; they can swim 6-9 km/h (4-6 mph) for up to 160 km (100 miles).

Polar bears can swim for days at a time. They use their broad hind legs as rudders while paddling with their front paws.

•••

It is estimated that there are around 26,000 wild polar bears living today.

•••

There are around 19 subpopulations of polar bears living in the Arctic circle.

•••

Polar bears are the world's largest land predators. When standing tall, they can reach more than 11 ft (3.35 m).

Under their fur, polar bears have black skin. Their coat is transparent, and only appears white because of the light it reflects back.

...

Their black skin helps absorb the sunlight and keep them warm.

...

There is so much vitamin A in a polar bear's liver that if a human were to eat it, they would die.

Despite their size, polar bears can jump up to eight feet (2.4 m) out of the water if they want to scare a seal.

• • •

Polar bears aren't fast enough to catch seals in open water, so they use ice blocks as hunting platforms to surprise and attack their prey.

• • •

Polar bears will often wait very still for hours at known seal breathing holes to catch them.

Photo by Hans-Jurgen Mager on Unsplash

Female polar bears give birth to their cubs in snow dens, which helps to protect newborns from the harsh cold.

. . .

The female polar bear will dig between 3-9 ft (1-3 m) into the snow to make her den. It usually consists of a long tunnel leading to a larger chamber. Inside, the temperature is typically several degrees warmer than outside.

. . .

Polar bear cubs are usually born between November and December.

When they are born, polar bear cubs are around 12 in (30 cm) in size and weigh just 17 oz. (500 g).

• • •

Although they start small, cubs grow quickly thanks to their mother's milk, which is 35 per cent fat.

• • •

Cubs emerge from their dens when they are around four or five months old. Then, for the next two years, they learn to hunt with their mothers before heading off on their own.

When a polar bear gets dirty, it gives itself a snow bath! By rolling around in the ice and snow, they clean off any dirt to make sure their fur is soft and matt-free, making it better for insulation.

. . .

Approximately two-thirds of polar bear litters are twins. It is rare for them to have more than two cubs.

. . .

Polar bears have huge paws—up to 11.81 in (30 cm) across. These help spread their weight more evenly when crossing thin patches of ice.

On the bottom of the polar bear's paws are small bumps called papillae. These provide grip while walking on slippery ice.

. . .

Polar bears are very polite! For example, before sharing food with another bear, they ask for permission by touching their noses together.

. . .

Polar bears have home ranges rather than territories. This means they may share their home range with many other polar bears and are not territorial over their space.

The size of a polar bear's home range varies dramatically. Some are as large as the state of California, while others may be as small as a single fjord.

...

Approximately 60 per cent of the world's polar bear population lives in Canada.

...

Polar bears don't mind when the weather is a little bit warmer, but they can overheat during summers when temperatures may reach up to 68°F (20°C). They roll in the snow to cool down.

On land, polar bears can reach speeds of up to 40km/h (25 mph).

• • •

Most polar bears live between 11-18 years, but some (particularly those in captivity) survive until they are over 30 years old.

• • •

On average, a female polar bear will have five litters of cubs over her lifetime.

**Polar bear mother with two cubs waiting
on a snowy patch in northern Alaska.**
Image: Hans-Jurger Mager

The polar bear's scientific name is *Ursus maritimus*, which translates to 'sea bear'.

· · ·

There are eight species in the same family (*Ursidae*) as polar bears: American black bear, Asian black bear, brown bear, giant panda, spectacled bear, sun bear and sloth bear.

· · ·

There are many different names for polar bears. For example, the Inuit people of Canada call them *nanuq*. In Russia, they are called *beliy medved*, and in Norway and Greenland, they are called *isbjorn*.

While polar bears could probably survive in Antarctica, the local animals wouldn't be so lucky. They have evolved to have no land predators, so many species could be wiped out if polar bears were there.

. . .

Like dogs, polar bears have non-retractable claws, which help them grip onto the ice better.

. . .

The oldest polar bear fossils ever found were from Svalbard in northern Norway. They date back 115,000–130,000 years — before the last ice age.

International Polar Bear Day is held on the 27th of February each year. This day is used to spread awareness about the problems polar bears face, particularly surrounding global warming.

. . .

Polar bears are mostly solitary (except when breeding) but have been known to occasionally hang around in small groups. A group of polar bears is called a sleuth.

. . .

Polar bears have amazing memories and can recognise other bears they have met in the past.

Polar bears have shrunken in size since the 20th century. Scientists believe this is because there is less food available.

. . .

Polar bears do not hibernate. However, they may build a snow den to help stay warm during the winter. Their breathing and other body functions may slow down to preserve energy, too.

. . .

While a female polar bear is pregnant, she may stay in her den for up to three months without eating anything. She lives off of her fat reserves.

Polar bears generally mate during April. Male polar bears will walk long distances to find a cub-less female.

. . .

When cubs are born, they are almost hairless and completely blind.

. . .

When a female is pregnant, she can double in weight up to 1,100 lb (500 kg)!

. . .

Polar bears are one of the most sexually dimorphic mammals in the world. This means that males and females are very different, and it is easy to tell them apart.

After polar bear populations drastically dropped, an international treaty was established in 1973 that made hunting polar bears illegal, unless you are a native Inuit. Since then, polar bear numbers have been much higher.

...

Now, a new problem faces polar bears — climate change. In the last 20 years, the amount of ice at the ice caps has decreased by 15 per cent. As the ice gets smaller, polar bears have fewer opportunities to find food.

Another big threat to polar bears is oil and gas exploration in the Arctic. As big companies dig for these natural resources, the polar bears' habitat is being destroyed.

. . .

Around 300 polar bears live in zoos and aquariums around the world. However, many conservationists believe polar bears shouldn't be kept in zoos as they can't provide them with the space and conditions that they need to be happy.

There is much debate over whether Rupert the Bear is a brown bear or a polar bear! He was originally designed to be a brown bear, but they ended up printing him in white to save on printing costs.

. . .

The word 'Arctic' comes from the Greek word for 'bear' — 'Arktus'. This also means that technically, Antarctica translates to 'no bears'.

. . .

Polar bears have smaller heads and longer necks than other bears so that they can stick their noses into holes in the ice to find food.

Their long noses also help to warm up
the cold air on its way to their lungs.

. . .

Polar bears and brown bears have the
same bite force of 1200 lbs (544 kg), but
polar bears have longer and sharper
teeth.

. . .

All five countries where polar bears live
have signed the *International Agreement
on the Conservation of Polar Bears*,
an important treaty that is helping to
protect polar bears.

On rare occasions, polar bears have
swum from Greenland over to Iceland.

...

Despite being surrounded by it, polar
bears rarely drink water. Instead,
they get their water from the chemical
reaction that happens while they are
breaking down fat.

...

Polar bears have 42 teeth.

...

Polar bears are so well insulated that
they are almost invisible in infrared
photography.

As polar bears get older, their skin often turns more yellow. In captivity, they may also turn a greenish colour as algae start to grow and stain their fur.

. . .

Polar bears are pretty quiet animals, although they do have a few different sounds they use to communicate.

Females use moans and chuffs to communicate with their young, while bleats are used by cubs when they are in distress. Growls and roars are used as a sign of aggression.

Polar bears leave scent markers along their tracks so that other bears can keep track of them.

. . .

The longest recorded non-stop swim a polar bear has ever made was 426 miles (685 km), (the distance of Washington D.C. to Boston!) over nine days. The female polar bear lost 22 per cent of her body weight during the journey.

. . .

Older polar bears will usually just eat the skin and blubber of a seal, which is easier to digest, while the younger bears eat the red meat.

During the late summer, polar bears
can go without food for several months.
During this time, when there is little or
no sea ice, polar bears can't catch any
seals, so they rely on their fat reserves.

• • •

Female polar bears have been known to
adopt abandoned cubs as their own.

• • •

Females can start breeding when they
are four years old (or five years old in
the Beaufort Sea area).

The polar bear is an apex predator. This means that it is at the top of the food chain in its habitat.

· · ·

Although polar bears technically have no predators, they have occasionally been taken by orca whales. However, polar bears are smart and won't enter the water if they sense an orca in the area.

· · ·

In parts of Canada, brown bears and polar bears are often seen in the same areas, mostly fighting over carcasses.

Indigenous people, such as Inuits, have hunted polar bears for centuries.

They have a use for every part of the body — the fur for clothing and warmth, the fat for fuel, the gallbladder and heart for creating medicines and the tendons as a thread for clothing.

. . .

It is believed that polar bears became a species 400,000-600,000 years ago when they diverged from the brown bear. The brown bear is their closest relative.

The Inuit and native Alaskan
people tell many folklore stories
about polar bears. A common one is
that polar bears are humans when they
are inside their homes, and put on bear
hides when they go outdoors.

• • •

Polar bears do the 'doggy paddle' when
they swim.

• • •

Debby the polar bear was the oldest
known polar bear, living to the age of
42. She lived in the Assiniboine Park
Zoo in Winnipeg until 2008.

If you want to see polar bears on the TV and in books, there are lots of great options — animated and real. Television show *Noah's Island*, the novel *East*, and the book/animated film *The Bear* are all popular among polar bear fans.

. . .

One of the mascots at the Sochi 2014 Winter Olympics was a polar bear named Bely Mishka.

. . .

Coca-Cola has used polar bears in its marketing for years. You can even buy merchandise at their official store featuring the polar bears, such as phone covers and clothing.

The U.S. Geological Survey has estimated that the world's population of polar bears will decrease by half by 2050, due to the shrinking of the ice caps.

• • •

There are lots of ways that you can help to raise awareness about the problems polar bears face. Through associations such as *Polar Bears International* and the *WWF*, you can adopt a polar bear and find out lots of other ways that you can help. We have more tips coming up!

POLAR BEARS: CONSERVATION

Sadly, polar bears are a threatened species and they are facing serious threats due to climate change and human activities. The melting sea ice is making it harder for them to find food and a place to raise their young.

Some polar bear populations are hunted by indigenous peoples for food and cultural reasons, and overhunting can be a problem if it is not done sustainably.

HOW CAN YOU HELP?

There are lots of ways you can help protect the future of polar bears. There are organisations, such as the WWF, Polar Bears International, and the Polar Bear Specialist Group that work with polar bears. But you don't need to be a scientist to help polar bears. We can all play a role in protecting these amazing creatures and their habitat.

JUST A FEW WAYS YOU CAN HELP:

- Adopt or sponsor a polar bear;
- Raise money in your community or at school for polar bear conservation projects;
- On your birthday or a special occasion, ask for donations to a polar bear conservation organisation in your name instead of gifts;
- Share messages on your social media and talk to friends and family about the problems polar bears face;
- Using less electricity, recycling and eating less meat can all help prevent climate change.

International Polar Bear Day is celebrated each year on February 27, and it's another great opportunity to spread awareness about them.

POLAR BEAR QUIZ

Now test your knowledge in our Polar Bear Quiz! Answers can be found on page 77.

1 How many teeth does a polar bear have?

2 What type of mammal are polar bears defined as?

3 In which countries do polar bears live?

4 What are male and female polar bears called?

5 Polar bears are the largest species of bear. True or false?

6 What is a hybrid between a grizzly bear and a polar bear called?

7 How many polar bears do scientists think are living in the wild at the moment?

8 How many subpopulations of polar bears are there?

9 What colour is a polar bear's skin?

10 How do polar bears catch seals?

11 Where do female polar bears give birth?

12 During which months are polar bear cubs usually born?

13 Female polar bears usually give birth to how many cubs in a litter?

14 What percentage of the world's polar bear population lives in Canada?

15 What is the scientific name for a polar bear?

16 When is International Polar Bear Day?

17 Polar bears hibernate. True or false?

18 What are the biggest threats to polar bear populations?

19 How can you tell that a polar bear is old?

20 How long does a female stay in her den while waiting for cubs to be born?

A polar bear mother feeding her cubs.

ANSWERS

1. 42

2. Marine mammals.

3. Canada, Russia, USA (Alaska), Greenland and Norway.

4. Boars and sows.

5. True.

6. A pizzly bear, or a grolar bear.

7. 26,000.

8. 19.

9. Black.

10. By waiting on ice blocks near seal breathing holes.

11. In snow dens.

12. November and December.

13. Two.

14. 60%.

15. *Ursus maritimus.*

16. 27th February

17. False.

18. Oil and gas exploration, and climate change.

19. Their fur is usually yellower.

20. Up to three months.

Polar Bear
WORD SEARCH

Can you find all the words below in the word search puzzle on the left?

ARCTIC	**SEALS**	**BOAR**
POLAR BEAR	**MARINE**	**BLUBBER**
CUBS	**GLACIER**	**FURRY**

SOLUTION

				S							
		M			E					G	
		A				A				L	
F	U	R	R	Y			L			A	
		I		C				S		C	
		N		U	T					I	
		E		B		I				E	
				S		C				R	
	B										
	P	O	L	A	R	B	E	A	R		
			A		B	L	U	B	B	E	R
			R								

SOURCES

"Top 10 Facts About Polar Bears". 2021. WWF. *https://www.wwf.org.uk/learn/fascinating-facts/polar-bears.*

"10 Facts About Polar Bears! | National Geographic Kids". 2014. National Geographic Kids. *https://www.natgeokids.com/uk/discover/animals/general-animals/polar-bear-facts/.*

"7 Surprising Polar Bear Facts - Polar Bears International". 2021. Polarbearsinternational.Org. *https://polarbearsinternational.org/news/article-polar-bears/7-surprising-polar-bear-facts/.*

"10 Fast Facts About Polar Bears". 2016. Arctic Kingdom. *https://arctickingdom.com/10-fast-facts-polar-bears/.*

"Why Do Polar Bears Have White Fur? And Nine Other Polar Bear Facts". 2021. World Wildlife Fund. *https://www.worldwildlife.org/stories/why-do-polar-bears-have-white-fur-and-nine-other-polar-bear-facts.*

"Polar Bear - Wikipedia". 2021. En.Wikipedia.Org. *https://en.wikipedia.org/wiki/Polar_bear.*

Facts, Animal. 2021. "Polar Bear Guide: Where They're Found, What They Eat, And Why They're Threatened". Discover Wildlife. *https://www.discoverwildlife.com/animal-facts/mammals/facts-about-polar-bears/.*

"10 Amazing Facts About Polar Bears". 2020. Popular Mechanics. *https://www.popularmechanics.com/science/animals/g31004185/polar-bear-facts/?slide=9.*

"Polar Bear". 2021. Young People's Trust For The Environment. *https://ypte.org.uk/factsheets/polar-bear.*

"Polar Bear Facts & Conservation - Polar Bears International". 2021. Polarbearsinternational.Org. *https://polarbearsinternational.org/.*

"Famous Polar Bears - Polar Bear Facts And Information". 2021. Polarbear-World.Com. *https://www.polarbear-world.com/famous-polar-bears/.*

"Debby (Polar Bear) - Wikipedia". 2021. En.Wikipedia.Org. *https://en.wikipedia.org/wiki/Debby_(polar_bear).*

"13 Facts You Didn't Know About Polar Bears". 2021. Destination Nunavut. *https://www.destinationnunavut.ca/discover/13-facts-you-didnt-know-about-polar-bears.*

Your feedback means the world to us, and we kindly ask you to share your thoughts with a review on whichever platform you purchased this book.

Not only do your words bring us joy, but they also guide fellow readers in choosing the perfect book for them.

Thanks again for your support!

If you'd like to learn more about other exciting animals visit us at:
www.bellanovabooks.com

ALSO BY JENNY KELLETT

... and more!

Available at

www.bellanovabooks.com

and all major online bookstores.